WRITINGS OF A YOUNG GIRL

Written by Josie Monahan
Illustrated by Rebecca Green

Printed July, 2013

"For my Papa who inspires me and made this book possible.
And for young and old readers alike..."

- ***Josie***

First printing: July 2013

ISBN: 978-1-939625-41-0

Library of Congress Control Number: 2013909660

Published by Inkwell Productions
10869 N. Scottsdale Road # 103-128
Scottsdale, AZ 85254-5280

Tel. 480-315-3781
E-mail info@inkwellproductions.com
Website www.inkwellproductions.com

Printed in the United States of America

Endorsements

"Simply, I cannot put ***Writings of a Young Girl*** down. Similar to ***I'll Love You Forever*** and ***Good Night Moon*** this author, did I mention she's ten, speaks right to my heart. She will yours too. Buy plenty of copies, this is a book you will want to give to every young and old reader alike."

~ ***Cindy Zimmermann, International Columnist**, Pen World Magazine, Author, A Woman of Interest, Founder, Writing in Style.*

"In her first book, ***Writings of a Young Girl***, 10-year old Josie Monahan invites all children and adults to take the time to read about her world, and then step into their own. Like the first kiss of an April shower, Josie sends us one drop at a time. A touch of love. We feel it, hear it, and our imaginations takes over, lured by life's realities, feelings, and the excitement of our own discoveries that will shape our lives forever.

Josie, still young enough to express her thoughts with the innocence of child magic, welcomes readers to her world where cats write, squirrels scamper, and a bunny listens to the far away sounds of a lawn mower. At the same time she urges readers to think about the stars, birds clouds and snow on their own journey's. Every poem, every phrase, every creature in Josie's life evokes emotion. We want this for our children and ourselves too. This is one young writer whose heart beats with warm feelings in rhythm with the world."

~ ***Penny Porter** Author: Heart Strings and Tail Tuggers, Adobe Secrets and several children's books. President emeritus: The Society of Southwestern Authors.*

"Since Josie was 6 years old, I would find little scraps of paper in her room, under tables, around the house...with little bits of wisdom or poems written on them. I would always ask, where did you hear this, thinking surely these ideas, this depth of feeling could never have come from a child this young. The answer was always a shrug and a casual, "I dunno...I just thought it." I started saving these little bits of reflection and insight (can a child really have insight with so little experience in life??) and creative writings. Writings of a Young Girl contains her thoughts on life and gives a unique view of what's important in relationships with our friends, our world and ourselves...all from the eyes of a child."

~ ***Laura Monahan***

About the Author

Josie Monahan, who is nine years old at this writing, began making up stories with her grandmother when she was two while riding a wooden horse she named Princess. These stories often continued for a half hour or more and were never the same. She used words like veterinarian, venom and shied. Her stories were always happy stories. As birthdays passed, her vocabulary grew and her stories became more complex. When she was nine, she auditioned and was accepted into the Children's Choir in the Michigan Opera Theatre. She appears as an actress and singer in a local theater group. She enjoys competing in swimming, volleyball and softball. Sensitive, caring and always smiling, Josie's greatest joy comes from the many friendships she has formed.

PART 1:
POEMS

I AM SPECIAL, I AM ME

I am as smart as an ape learning sign language in a special class. I am as athletic as a cheetah ready for a tasty lunch. I am as creative as an artist painting a mural to be seen by millions of different eyes. I am as kind as a mouse to a cat wishing not to be painfully devoured. I am as determined as a duck with lots of ducklings in front of a speeding car by a pond. I am as flexible as an acrobat gracefully flipping through the air. I am as strong as an elephant with his memory of finding the ancient water hole. I am as compassionate as a lady who has found a baby on her doorstep. I am as friendly as a baby bunny who sniffs me. I am as funny as a panda sneezing in a dusty bamboo forest. I am as special as a purple apple in a bucket full of green apples.

**Josie wrote these words all around a drawing of herself, the words weaving their way around her body. Second Grade, 2009, Age 7.*

The Beautiful Book of Nature

A LEAF
Blows through the wind
Silently while the clouds
Pass by

A BABY BUNNY
Slowly wakes up from a nap
While Suzy is just closing
Her eyes soothed by the
Sound of a far away lawn
Mower on a hot summer day

A CRANE
Stands as a tree with
Her vision into the water
Hunting for fish

A STARFISH
Crawling off in the
Ocean water in the
Islands of Jamaica

A SQUIRREL
Scampering from tree to tree
On a sunny afternoon in
The beautiful park of birch trees

A CATERPILLAR
Creeps along the fence
Near Lolo's garden
Enjoying the hot sun

A LAMB
Being herded with its
Mother eats fresh green grass
While skipping along the Alps

A GIRAFFE
Grazes slowly among
The Savannahs in Africa

A SEAGULL
Swoops above the sparkling
White beach which has lots
Of sparkling ocean water

And above them all
Sits the sparkling
Stars which light up
Our world in which we
Live together.

2009, Age 6.

"OUR WORLD
IN WHICH WE
LIVE TOGETHER"

HELLO

Good day sunshine, warm as a fuzzy white blanket. Always popping out of the Earth. Your birds chirping, singing songs. A brand new violet every day. You always cheer me up when your flowers poke out. Brightness, warmness, so much amusement! Jumping, running, picking flowers. I never go inside, I'm always too busy enjoying everything around me. Spring, you're like finding wonderful new treats in the fridge at night.

GOODBYE

Farewell snow, as blank as white boards. Never waking, constantly sleeping. You're like ice cream without sprinkles or a cone. Your icy cold winds give me a chill. Snow is a blanket covering everything up, everything bright, warm and new.

**The teacher gave each student a sheet of paper with HELLO printed on one side and GOODBYE on the other. Her instructions were to finish the thoughts. 2012, Age 9.*

Part 2: Short Stories

THE DAY OF THE BLACK FOG

It was a cool Spring day and Ella was outside skipping along with the wind and picking daisies. She loved to pick daisies and make long, long daisy chains. After about an hour, the sky turned grey. Then after another hour it turned black. Finally the blackness stretched down until it was all the way to the ground. Ella was petrified! She sprinted back down the steep hill to her home. She burst inside.

"Mom! Dad! What is that!?"

"That's the black fog, honey. It comes every thirty years and it won't hurt you."

"Really?" Asked Ella.

"Yes, dearest," her parents said.

"Well I'm going to catch some of it," she said.

She marched out the door and tried but didn't succeed.

Finally, she trusted the fog and loved it.

2010, Age 7.

Clover

Tables being knocked over, green flashes everywhere, doors off their hinges. It's the night of March 16th and leprechauns are everywhere! On that night, a small, dark shadow bounded through the grass. Who could it be but Clover the leprechaun? "Creeeeeeaaaaaaaaak", went the door. "Pit pat pit pat pit pat", went the tiniest little feet you could ever imagine. "This family will wake up to a big surprise," laughed Clover. Now this was a great plan!

The little leprechaun snuck from shadow to shadow, always alert. "Slam! Crash! Boom!" Couches, chairs, even tables were either on their sides or strewn across the room. "Oh no! Oh no! 'What has happened to our house?' the family will cry out into the morning air. But as they look over the door step they will see 3 golden coins left by me!"

The cunning little leprechaun continued his work, spilling milk, ripping down curtains, and taking down pictures. Clover of course made sure to keep the family asleep, with a little bit of magic.

When his work was done, he helped himself to some ice cream in the freezer. Then out the door went the jolly little leprechaun, to go into hiding until next year when again he will make his special visit to a special house, on the night of March 16th!

2012, Age 9.

THOUGHTS ON A STICKY NOTE

WHEN I GO AWAY
I HAVE A WIND
THAT WILL CARRY ME HOME
THAT WILL CARRY ME HOME
THAT WILL CARRY ME HOME,
PAST THE FIR TREES
AND THROUGH THE STREAMS
THE WIND WILL CARRY
ME HOME.

2010

TRUE FRIENDS
CAN HEAR YOU
WHEN YOU SPEAK
WITHOUT WORDS.

OUT OF MY WINDOW I
SEE A CLEAR, WHITE-BLUE SKY
WITH NO CLOUDS. TREES,
STANDING TALL, BARE TO THE
BONE. OUT OF MY WINDOW
I SEE WINTER,
CALLING ME TO COME OUT
SO HE CAN PUT HIS ICY
HAND ON MY SHOULDER.

A GOOD BOOK CAN MAKE
YOU LAUGH
BUT IT CAN ALSO MAKE
YOU CRY.

The Love of Horses

Chapter 1.

Once upon a time there lived a girl named Lily. Lily was eight years old. She had two friends named Lucy and Lila. They called themselves the "L" Group. One day they met after school and Lily said, "Hey, who here wants to ride a horse?" They all shouted together in delight, "I do!" "Well then let's go ask our moms," said Lily. So one by one they went to each other's houses but they always got the same answer. "You're only eight girls. You can't take the long journey that you're supposed to take to be taught how to ride a horse." But every time they got the answer, they said together, "But mom." But the very last to answer was Lily's mom, she said, "Ok girls, but be careful." So off they went to start their journey. Halfway there, they became hungry. So they saw a store that sold scones and tea sandwiches. They went in and ate. The shop was called Little Treats.

Chapter 2.

The girls kept walking. Pretty soon, they saw a man raking leaves. They went over to ask him for directions. Lucy said, "Excuse me, do you know how to get to the Western Rodeo?" The man said, "Go straight up ahead and you'll see a cherry blossom tree. Turn right then left then left again. You'll see it right ahead...By the way, my name is Leo Asorman and you know what? I can talk to animals! And you know I'll be with you all the time! Okay, now run along. You'd better hurry before it gets dark." So the girls had dinner at a Japanese restaurant. After the girls were done with dinner, they kept walking. Finally, they saw the cherry tree! So when they got to the cherry tree, they turned right... then left...then left again. And they saw the rodeo right ahead! They got there and a man said, "Need a room to sleep in before practice tomorrow? Room 236," and handed them a key. So they picked their beds...and read...and went to sleep. Because of course they had a long day tomorrow...and didn't know what was in store.

Chapter 3.

In the morning they took baby foals and named them Thunder, Twilight, and Starlight. When Lila first rode Thunder, he galloped, and jumped, and bucked. Lila thought this was enough for one day. Lily and Lucy agreed. They decided they would wait until they were nine before they went riding again.

2010, Age 7.

GORILLA

You've probably heard that a gorilla is dangerous and mean. Well think again. Gorillas are very peaceful and kind. In this report, you will learn all about the gorilla, including why they are endangered. I hope you find the gorilla to be as interesting as I do.

The Gorilla is a very strong and beautiful creature that belongs to the mammal group. Females are four ft. tall and males are up to six ft. Females usually weight between 154 and 250 lbs. Males weigh up to 350 lbs. All gorillas' arms are longer than their legs. In zoos, they usually live from 40 to 50 years. The head of a male mountain gorilla is higher and more pointed, and his nose has a wider gap in the middle. Lowland males often have a patch of red hair on their heads and mountain gorillas do not.

The three different types of gorillas all live in Africa. The Mountain gorillas live in the mountains (of course). The Eastern Lowland gorillas live in the Eastern lowlands (of course). Finally, the Western Lowland gorillas live in the Western lowlands. Most of the gorillas that you see in the zoos are Western Lowlands. Well, it is true. They do live in Africa.

Food wise, the gorilla is mostly an herbivore. They eat leaves, nuts, roots, flowers, etc. I predict that gorillas would be good hunters because of their similarity to humans. But they are plant eaters so that will probably never happen. There is not a lot of information on where the gorilla is on the food chain. My hypothesis is that they are near the top. So over all, gorillas are versions of humans waiting to develop.

You have probably wondered why the gorilla is endangered. Well it is because of disappearing habitats and gorillas are being used to make medicine. Baby gorillas are mostly used to make medicine because they make the exact right amount. I really hope that gorillas will not become endangered soon because they are wonderful animals. There is not a lot more information on why the gorilla is endangered.

In conclusion, I hope you have enjoyed my report and learned all about the gorilla. I love gorillas and hope they will become more common soon. They are very interesting animals as you can see.

2011, Age 8.

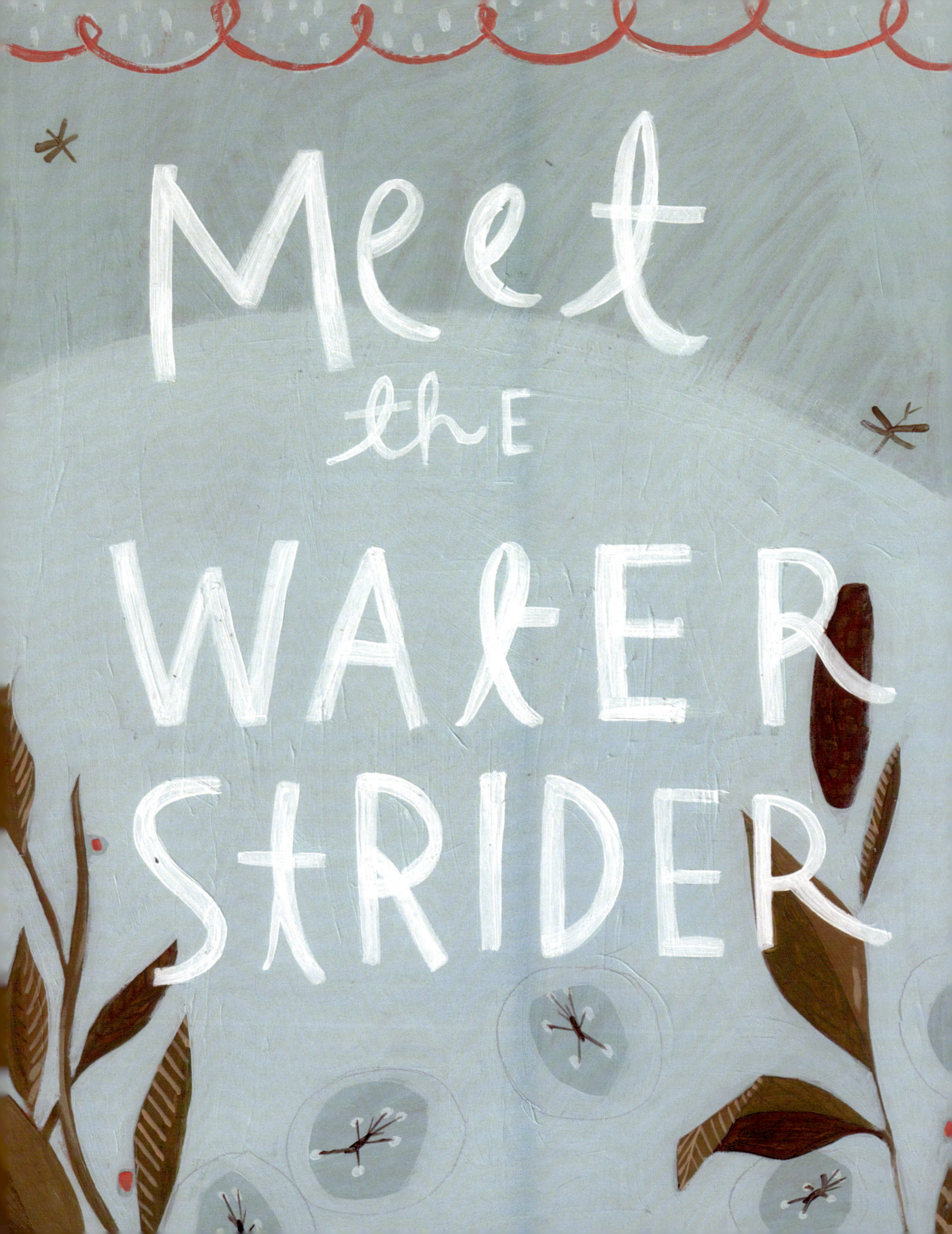
Meet the Water Strider

INTRODUCTION

Picture yourself water skiing. The wind is blowing in your face with ocean spray. That's what a Water Strider does every day, except without skis or a boat. Water Striders are truly amazing creatures. Find out why in this article.

Water Striders never ever bite humans!

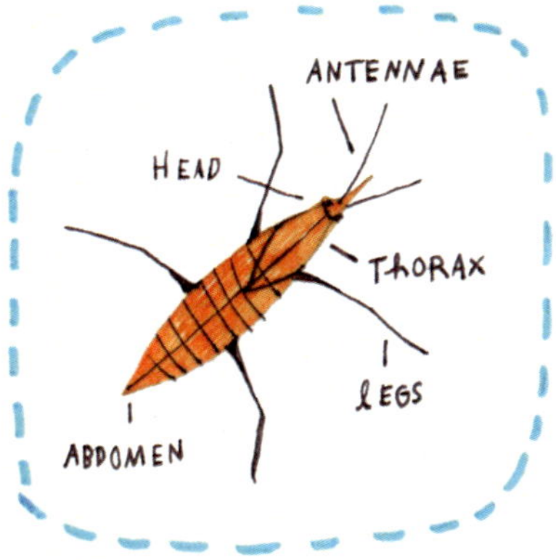

The hair on a water bug's leg can be seen if they are out of the water.

NO DANGER HERE

The Water Strider isn't very dangerous or harmful unless you are a bug! The odds of a Water Strider biting a human…0! What the Strider eats are small bugs that fall onto the surface of the water. They usually feed on tadpoles, small fish, and salamanders.

Stretch!

SUPER BUG

The water bug's talents are endless! The bug known as the Water Strider can often be seen walking on the surface of the water. They can use their middle legs to push them on the water while they steer with their front legs. The water strider also uses its front legs to catch prey. For example a Water Strider could eat an injured bug if it fell into the water.

HOMEY INSECT HOMES

I bet you would hate living where a Water Strider lives. I know I would! Water Striders live in quiet coves and small protected ponds and lakes. But, they can also burrow into mud if their habitat dries up and becomes dormant. They can go into small streams and ditches as well.

DINNER TIME

Mmm, yummy: Water Striders feed on Salamanders and small fish.
To get their dinner, they simply stride along the water and grasp their prey in their front legs. For a Strider dinner is the most important meal of the day.

WOWIE!!

A Water Strider could fit in at a circus! A Strider's legs make tiny dents in the water like skis. They can move very fast as they skim over the water. The oily hairs on the ends of its legs repel water and also trap air to help keep the Water Strider afloat.

**The assignment was to write a magazine article with captions on a bug of your choice. 2010, Age 8.*

TRAPPED!

The scratching of pencils on paper was everywhere. The clicking of pens and the whooshing of high lighters and markers were also in the air.

"The sound of writing is music to my ears," Mrs. Chandler chimed.

"Scratch, Scratch, Tap," was the only response she got.

Ell, Donna, and Scarlet were sitting in their favorite writing spot in the whole classroom. The back of the room where they slipped when no one was looking. It was perfect, complete with three beautiful desks, cushions, pencil holders, and sharpeners.

The girls were writing, when suddenly, their heads dropped onto the desks and their eyes began to close.

"RIIIINNG!"

Hearing the faint sound, Ell began to open her eyes.

"Donna, Scarlet, wake up!" Ell yelled frantically.

"Wh-where are we?" Donna and Scarlet both asked sleepily.

"We're at school, ALONE!" Ell shouted the last word.

"N-No, that can't be!" Scarlet stuttered.

"Well, actually, there's no denying, we're stuck at school." Donna clarified.

"Okay! Everyone calm down ," Ell commanded. Scarlet and Donna sank into their chairs.

"All we have to do is bang on the doors and maybe someone will hear us," Ell guessed hopefully.

"It's worth a try," Scarlet muttered, shrugging.

So the girls paced step by step to the front doors. They raised their hands and made a big fist. "Bang, bang, bang, bang, bang," went the door as it got knocked.

"No luck," Donna sighed, as an angry Ell paced around in circles.

"There's got to be a way." Ell scrabbled through her brain.

"Um, oh," she thought. "The janitor's closet!" She exclaimed.

"What about it?" Scarlet groaned.

"We can get a tool and break out."

"Oh yeah!" The girls yelled.

They sprinted as fast as they could. Ell snatched the door open. All she saw were brooms and brushes.

"Rats," she muttered.

"Well, the least we can do is get some fresh air," Donna said.

So the girls persuaded themselves to go to the Nature Center. They then saw a green thing moving. Not any green thing, the janitor!

"Mr. Janitor, let us out!" The girls shouted.

That's just what he did. So the girls never fell asleep in school again.

2010, Age 7.

MOUNTAIN OF DEATH

Tiny, sleek cars and trucks rushed beneath me. My arms were wet with sweat.

"Wow," I said. "It is so cool to be up -"

Whoosh! Before I could finish, I felt a tug on the back of my shirt and soon I was being pulled from the edge of the mountain.

"Don't you dare go that close ever again!" She snapped.

As we kept walking I saw two men standing about three yards apart.

"They see something," my mom muttered, nervously.

"Four foot rattler!" One of the men shouted.

My brother was shaking. My mom grabbed his shirt and stepped forward, but I felt a burst of joy. I love snakes, I thought. A snake was slithering up the rock. We walked past. A few paces later, we saw a lizard sunning on a rock. A shiver ran down my back because I knew what it was.

"It - It's a G-Gila monster," I stuttered. My teeth were chattering. I was horrified, but I still held up my camera and snapped a picture.

"Click."

Then slowly, step by step, I walked past, staring at the monster all the time.

"Okay," my mom said, obviously worrying. "We are not going any further without your father here."

"Fine," I sighed. I turned around and started leaping down the mountain. I hopped into the car.

"Wow," I thought. "I sure am glad to be off *that* mountain."

2010, Age 7.

Little Vocabulary Story

Whose job is it to protect the everlasting circle of life? Animals in the jungle, in the ocean, in the sky? How do they live? Is it in their irreplaceable habitats? Maybe their bodies are trained to fight, to live out there like a machine. How do they go a whole day in wild places? Do they have a secret language to communicate? Do they travel together in the night? Do they travel at the top of the forest or at the bottom? Do they have a lot of energy? How do they live completely in comfort all the time?

**The teacher asked her students to write a paragraph or so using all the new vocabulary words they had learned that week. 2011, Age 9.*

PART: 3

THOUGHTFUL WRITINGS

A LETTER FROM OLIVER

**In 2011, Oliver the family cat passed away. Everyone had a good cry. But Josie's mother was the most distraught. Josie was concerned so the next morning she asked if she could go outside for some fresh air. It was raining. A few minutes later she returned with a damp envelope and a crudely written note from Oliver. She has never admitted that she wrote the note. When her six-year-old brother, Mac, saw the note he said, "I certainly hope that the next cat we get can write."*

BIRTHDAY CARDS

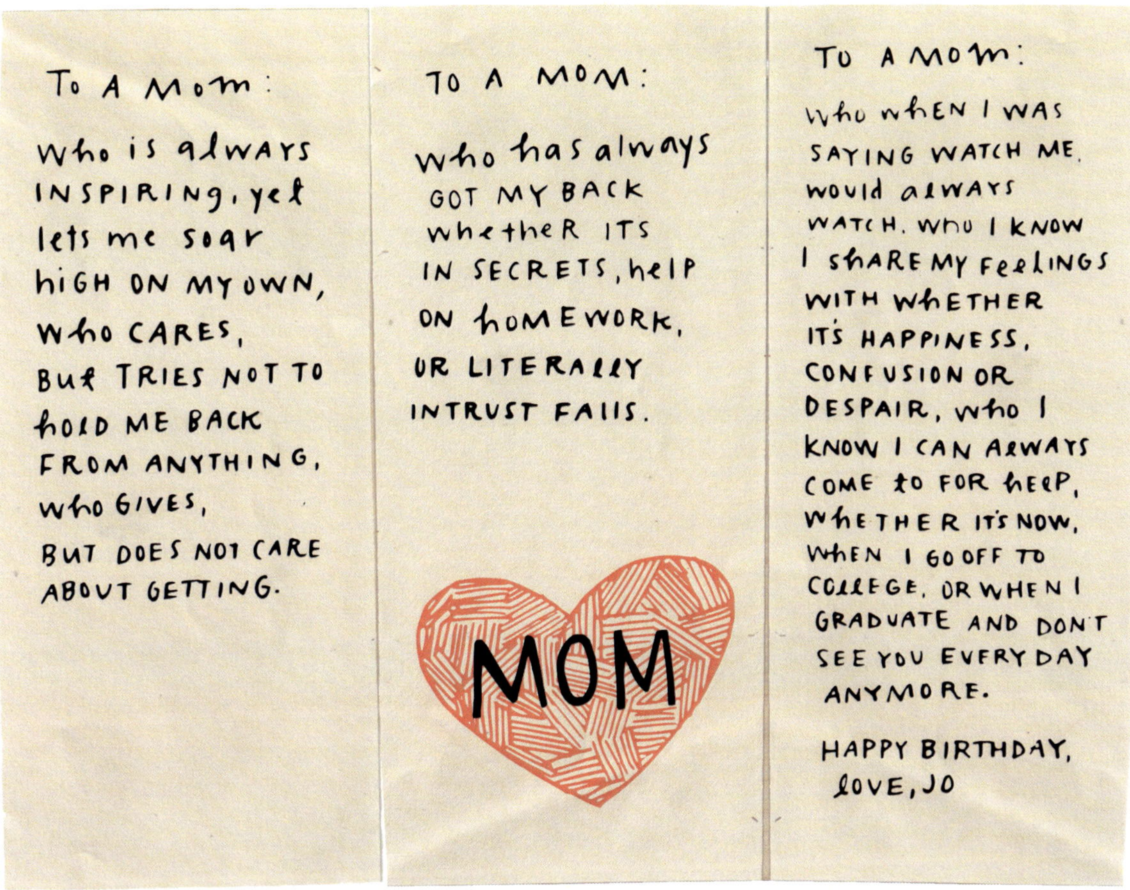

TO A MOM:

Who is always INSPIRING, yet lets me soar high ON MY OWN, Who CARES, But TRIES NOT TO hold ME BACK FROM ANYTHING, who GIVES, BUT DOES NOT CARE ABOUT GETTING.

TO A MOM:

Who has always GOT MY BACK whether ITS IN SECRETS, help ON homEWORK, OR LITERALLY INTRUST FALLS.

MOM

TO A MOM:

Who when I WAS SAYING WATCH ME, would always WATCH. Who I KNOW I SHARE MY FEELINGS WITH WHETHER IT'S HAPPINESS, CONFUSION OR DESPAIR, who I KNOW I CAN ALWAYS COME to FOR HELP, WHETHER IT'S NOW, WHEN I GO OFF TO COLLEGE, OR WHEN I GRADUATE AND DON'T SEE YOU EVERY DAY ANYMORE.

HAPPY BIRTHDAY,
love, JO

2012, Age 9.

2011, Age 8.

Why I love the Holidays

There is a reason why Christmas makes me smile. Every year, my family goes to visit my grandparents in Arizona. It usually isn't very cold in the Southwest, so I can run around without a coat on. When I walk into my grandparents' house, I feel very happy. As I step in, I see a HUGE Christmas tree, all decorated and shining. I smell cookies (fresh-baked), caramel suckers (made by my grandpa) and roses (from the garden). Usually I go straight to my room to unpack, and then my grandparents have us hunt for presents. We have lots of fun, and then when dinner comes, we have a feast. I get to stay up late because it is Christmas. I feel good because I know I get to stay here for another week and a half.

Finally, I lumber off to bed and close my eyes as soon as my head hits the pillow. I can feel myself smiling all night.

**The Wayne County Community College sponsored a writing contest for all the grade schools in the Grosse Pointe district. The subject: Why I Love the Holidays. Each student who entered wrote their essay in school during free time. Josie was one of the winners. Each winner was invited to ride on a fire engine during the Thanksgiving parade and their photograph was included in the weekly community newspaper.*

THE ANGER JAR

One morning Mac was very upset and extremely angry. Josie tried to comfort her brother and in doing so invented The Anger Jar. Josie explained that when you are angry, you reach into the jar and take out a note which will help you get over your anger. Notes included such things as 'Go for a bike ride'or 'Visit a friend.'

2010, Age 8.

the ANGER jar
When you're ANGRY, come HERE
GO FOR A BIKE RIDE!
PLAY YOUR FAVORITE INSTRUMENT.

PART 4:
SONGS

Welcome to My World

Welcome to my world...sunshine, sunshine
You're the welcome to my world.
You bring peace down to Earth, yeah.
1,2,3,4, I can't count up anymore.
I just can't stand up any taller.
You're the welcome to my world.
Hey, hey, heeeey, hey, heeeey.
I just can't count up anymore.
You're the welcome to my world...yeah.

2010, Age 7.

Pets

Friends, you may keep for many years,
Family you will have for longer than you think.
Pets are a different story. They are waiting up above,
They will wait for us, as long as we need.
Companionship, loyalty will forever be between us.
It's just a blink of an eye before we are together
For eternity, for eternity,
We will run through fields in joy.
Play with me, laugh with me,
We will sing together now.

2011, Age 8.

My Life

Me and you are like a fusion in a smoothie (yeah).
Me and you,
I'm going to take you to
A special place that has hearts and diamonds
Every which way
It's a wedding, it's a wedding
And the most special thing that a wedding has
Is love.

2010, Age 7.

DREAMLAND FOREVER

When I lay down and close my eyes
Lots of pictures form in my head
Pixie fairies, candy trains
Forever in a dark blue sky.
Dreamland forever
Way out in the clouds.
Marshmallow bunnies, teddy bears,
Dreamland forever
Way out in the sky.
Dreamland, Dreamland, Dreamland, Dreamland
Way out in the clouds.

2009, Age 6.

the END

Just the BEGINNING!